A COMEDIAN IS SOMEONE WHO DOES IN A FEW SECONDS WHAT IT TAKES A CHICKEN HOURS TO ACCOMPLISH

But not to worry. You won't be laying any eggs with these 1001 razor-sharp one-liners that let you instantly prepare and swiftly serve up a feast of laughter.

Try them in your speech at the year-end company roast ... when making a snazzy new-product presentation for a client ... in a political rally campaign speech ... or any of the myriad occasions in which a public speaker needs to charm, relax, and capture the admiring attention of his or her audience.

Go ahead, try them—and spread some good-humored, side-splitting fun. Everyone loves—and needs—a good laugh!

1001 GREAT ONE-LINERS

JEFF ROVIN, a writer for *MAD* magazine, is the author of *1001 Great Jokes, 1001 More Great Jokes, TV Babylon, In Search of Trivia,* and *The Second Signet Book of Movie Lists* (all available in Signet editions).

1,001 GREAT ONE-LINERS

BY
JEFF ROVIN

A SIGNET BOOK

NEW AMERICAN LIBRARY

A DIVISION OF PENGUIN BOOKS USA INC.

NAL BOOKS ARE AVAILABLE AT QUANTITY DISCOUNTS
WHEN USED TO PROMOTE PRODUCTS OR SERVICES.
FOR INFORMATION PLEASE WRITE TO PREMIUM MARKETING DIVISION,
NEW AMERICAN LIBRARY, 1633 BROADWAY,
NEW YORK, NEW YORK 10019.

Copyright © 1989 by Jeff Rovin

SIGNET TRADEMARK REG. U.S. PAT. OFF. AND FOREIGN COUNTRIES
REGISTERED TRADEMARK—MARCA REGISTRADA
HECHO EN DRESDEN, TN, U.S.A.

SIGNET, SIGNET CLASSIC, MENTOR, ONYX, PLUME, MERIDIAN
and NAL BOOKS are published by New American Library, a division of
Penguin Books USA Inc., 1633 Broadway, New York, New York 10019

First Printing, November, 1989

1   2   3   4   5   6   7   8   9

PRINTED IN THE UNITED STATES OF AMERICA

INTRODUCTION

Great thinkers from Descartes to Jefferson to Captain Lou Albano have wrestled with the problem: What exactly is a one-liner?

To some, it's a coat with a single hunk of cloth to be zipped inside.

To others, it's a cruise agency with but one ship.

To still others, it's the only fib ever told by the Oscar-winning actor from *The Killing Fields*. (Surely you've heard of One-Lie Ngor?)

But to most, it's a short, often cutting remark.

This book is a collection of these curt, witty sayings. I mean, the precedent of publishing great humor books had already been set with New American Library's *1,001 Great Jokes* and *1,001 More Great Jokes*; there was no point in writing about coats, seagoing vessels, or Haing and his prevarication, fascinating though they would have been.

We hope you're not crushed, and that you will find this volume useful.

If you want a laugh, need a snide comment for a speech, or simply want to mess with your boss, spouse, or stockbroker, this is the book for you.

We've conveniently arranged the one-liners according to topic. There are over two hundred subjects in all; sort of a Ribster's Dictionary, if you will. What's more, there is extensive cross-referencing, which works this way: To the right of each topic, we've alphabetically listed subjects that are closely related. For example, if you look up OPTIMIST you'll be referred to PESSIMIST. Look up PLAYBOY, and you'll be told to turn to MACHISMO. Look up WOMEN, and you'll be guided to entries on FEMINISM, PROSTITUTES, STRIPPERS, WIDOWS, and others.

Following the main topic cross-references are listings with numbers after them: These refer to specific jokes under other headings. For example, DEATH and MOTHERS-IN-LAW might not seem to have much in common (especially if you aren't married). But if you're perusing the DEATH one-liners, you'll be referred to MOTHERS-IN-LAW 5, which deals with the demise of the titular lady.

We're sure you'll agree that this book deserves a Pulitzer Prize—or at least the kind discussed in LITERATURE 3.

In any case, we hope you'll have fun with it!

ACTORS

See CRITICS, FAME, MOTION PICTURES

1. Drunk actors are people who can't handle their boos.

2. A starlet is someone who makes her reputation by losing it.

3. The only thing most Broadway actors gain by going to Hollywood is three hours.

4. The reason so many actresses don't like playing Joan of Arc is that no matter how well they do, they end up getting fired.

ADVERTISING   *See* CLOTHING 7, TRAVEL 11

1. Advertising is a profession whose practitioners can put a good face on anything . . . except themselves.

2. An advertising executive is someone who dishes out baloney disguised as food for thought.

ALCOHOL

1. The problem with drinking to the health of others is that it ruins your own.

2. The difference between a pair of glasses and spectacles is the drinker's ability to hold his liquor.

3. The problem with most people who drink is that two pints make a quote.

4. Drinking doesn't drown your troubles, it simply irrigates them.

5. The difference between a drunk banker and a drunk woman is that one loses principal, the other principle.

6. Dignity is something that alcohol can't preserve.

7. The problem with alcoholics is that they would rather be good livers than have them.

8. Another problem is that not only do they drink to excess, they drink to anything.

9. If alcohol is bad for you, why do old drunks far outnumber old doctors?

10. There's nothing wrong with drinking like a fish, provided you drink what a fish drinks.

11. It never fails: Men who go out drinking leave fit as a fiddle, but come home tight as a drum.

12. A cocktail party is a place where drinks mix people.

13. A drunk is someone who goes into a bar optimistically, and leaves misty optically.

14. Alcoholics have this in common with arthritics: They're always stiff in one joint or another.

15. An alcoholic musician is someone who can't get past the first bar.

16. You know you have a drinking problem when you keep asking people for the time, and can't understand why you keep getting different answers.

17. Alcoholics are people who don't no when they've had enough.

18. Liquor is a substance that makes married men see double and feel single.

19. Unfortunately, the only way most people watch their drinking is when the bar has mirrors.

ALIMONY

See DIVORCE

1. How times change: Nowadays, a faithful husband is one whose alimony checks arrive on time.

2. A divorcee is a woman who gets richer by decrees.

3. Alimony is an arrangement in which two people make a mistake, but only one pays for it.

4. Paying alimony is the marital equivalent of having the TV on after you've fallen asleep.

5. It can also be described as bounty on the mutiny ...

6. ... or as bye now, pay later.

7. Most men find, in fact, that divorce is a matter of wife or debt.

8. A divorce costs more than a wedding, but it's worth it ...

9. ... even so, alimony is bound to give any man a splitting headache.

AMNESIA

See DISEASES, DOCTORS

1. A vicious circle: finding a cure for your amnesia, then forgetting what it is.

2. A doctor is someone who, when you complain about a memory loss, makes you pay in advance.

ANTIQUES

1. An antique is something your grandparents bought, your parents sold, and you bought again.

2. In most cases, though, antiques aren't what they're cracked up to be.

3. In fact, a common complaint heard in antique stores is that they just don't make 'em the way they used to.

4. The problem with antiques is that they leave you baroque.

5. Overall, what's the best you can hope to get from any antique shop? Remains to be seen.

APARTMENTS

See GAMBLING 8, INFLATION 3, 6, MISTRESSES 1

1. When the tenant failed to pay her rent, the landlord was upset and she was put out.

2. Nowadays, the only apartments most people can afford are those where you overlook the rent.

3. They call them high-rise apartments because that's exactly what the rent does.

ARGUMENTS

1. An argument is something you have when words flail you.

2. In most arguments, the bone of contention is the one between the ears.

3. The reason so many people have chips on their shoulders is because there's wood higher up.

ART

See MOTION PICTURES 2, 4

1. An artist is what anyone can claim to be, and no one can prove them wrong.

2. Artists are born ... which is the problem.

3. Modern art is to art what alphabet soup is to literature.

ASSUMPTIONS

1. Never "assume," or you'll make an "ass" of "u" and "me."

ASTROLOGY

1. A crisis: When your fortune cookie contradicts your horoscope.

AUCTIONS

1. An auction is a place where you can get something for nodding.

AUTOMOBILES

See COMMUTERS, DRUNK DRIVERS, MOBILE HOMES, MOTORCYCLES, TRAINS, SUMMERTIME 1, TEENAGERS 2, WOMEN 16

1. When it comes to cars, it's tough to drive a bargain.

2. Today, car sickness is what you get from looking at the sticker price.

3. Most cars have one part that desperately needs to be recalled: the nut behind the wheel.

4. The best advice any motorist can follow is to drive right so more pedestrians will be left.

5. Nowadays, the most common reason teenagers lose control of the car is that they can't make the payments.

6. Today, the only thing certain to last the life of a car are the payments.

7. An auto mechanic is someone you can always count on to fix your wagon.

8. All it takes is one long skid on the ice to convince a driver to retire.

9. This much is true about all motorists: Those with patience today are not patients tomorrow.

BABIES

See BIRTH-CONTROL, KIDS,
TEENAGERS, BIRDS 2, NUDISTS 6,
SEX 8

1. Many babies are descended from a long line ... which began on a date.

2. A baby is a person who must have bottle or bust.

3. A baby stroller is last year's fun on wheels.

4. A straight line is the shortest distance between a baby and anything breakable.

5. Two's company, three's the result.

BACHELORS

See CHAUVINISTS, GIGOLOS,
MACHISMO, PLAYBOYS

1. A bachelor is someone who's footloose and fiancee free.

2. He's also someone with an unalterable view of life ...

17

3. ... who adores women, though the feeling is never nuptial ...

4. ... who pulls off countless romances without a hitch ...

5. ... who makes it a practice to steer clear of women with bride ideas.

6. In fact, a bachelor's little black book is full of near Mrs.

7. He is simply someone who can't be miss-led.

8. And while married men may have better halves, bachelors have better quarters.

BANKRUPTCY See BANKS, FAILURES

1. The bankrupt are so unrepentent these days that they take a taxi to bankruptcy court, then ask the driver in as a creditor.

BANKS

See BANKRUPTCY, MONEY, THE STOCK MARKET, ALCOHOL 5, CHRISTMAS 4, 5

1. A bank is a place with a simple philosophy: no deposit, no return.

2. The reason money doesn't grow on trees is that banks own all the branches.

BASTARDS

See CONSCIENCE 3

1. A real bastard is someone who stabs you in the back, then has you arrested for carrying a concealed weapon.

2. Sometimes, though, he'll just pat you on the back to make sure you swallow what he's just told you . . .

3. . . . or pat you in the hope that you'll cough something up.

4. The problem is that, for every soul, you're bound to find a heel.

5. But at least all bastards have one redeeming feature: mortality.

BATHING SUITS   *See* BEAUTY, CLOTHING

1. Most women don't have the figure for a bikini, just the nerve.

2. The truth is, with the small amount of fabric going into bikinis these days, it's fair to refer to them as baiting suits.

3. Some designer bikinis are so alluring that women who try one on can hardly contain themselves.

4. The strange thing is, the more these bikinis cost, the less a woman gets for her money.

5. When buying a bikini, the less there is to speak of, the more there is to speak of.

6. In the final analysis, a bathing beauty is someone worth wading for.

BEAUTY

See BATHING SUITS, PLASTIC SURGERY, UGLINESS, WALLFLOWERS, SEX 7

1. A true beauty is someone with an exquisite profile ... all the way down.

2. A woman who's well painted isn't necessarily as pretty as a picture.

3. So many beautiful women have one thing guaranteed to knock your eyes out: a husband.

BIRDS

See CHICKENS

1. The reason birds chatter frantically in the morning is that their bills are over dew.

2. Sadly, the stork ends up being blamed for what is usually that fault of a lark.

BIRTH CONTROL

See BABIES, SEX

1. Birth control is a means of avoiding the issue.

BIRTHDAYS

See OLD AGE, MARRIAGE

1. A sure sign that you're getting on: When you try to blow out the candles on your birthday cake and the heat drives you back ...

2. ... when, by the time you've lit the last candle on your cake, the first one has burned out.

3. And you know you're not a kid anymore when the only thing you want for your birthday is not to be reminded of it.

BOATING

See FISHING, OPTIMISTS 2, TRAVEL 4, 5

1. Boats are never painted purple or pink, because if they collided, everyone would be marooned.

BOXING

See FOOTBALL, GOLF, SPORTS

1. A retired boxer is someone who's lost his jab.

2. Nowadays, the only way to make money hand over fist is to become a boxer.

BURLESQUE

See STRIPPERS

1. Burlesque is an art form that died out due to the lack of raw material.

BUSINESS   *See* EMPLOYERS, SALESPEOPLE, WORK, FEMINISTS 1, FLOWERS 5, MONEY 14, PERFUME 2

1. Most born executives are people with a parent who started the business.

2. The biggest guns in most corporations are those who have never been fired.

3. A business executive is someone who talks golf in the office and business on the golf course.

4. The problem with starting a monogram company is that it's difficult to have an initial success.

5. Likewise, founding a publishing company is tough: Not all books are bound to do well.

6. The reason so many businesses fail these days is that corporate chambers have too many bored members.

7. The trouble with starting a trash collection service is that you're always at people's disposal.

8. Without a doubt, the easiest undertaking to start from scratch is a flea circus ...

9. ... while the most difficult is a laundry. There's never a day without clothes competition.

10. In business, you can be on the right track, but if you don't move fast enough you'll still be run over.

11. A lumber yard is the only place where they're happy when business is come see, come saw.

12. In the end, of course, no customer is worse than no customers.

CAPITAL PUNISHMENT

See CRIME, DEATH, PRISONS 3

1. Capital punishment is the belief that the sword is mightier than the pen.

2. An electric chair is period furniture because it ends a sentence.

CARDS *See* GAMBLING 4, 7, MARRIAGE 13

1. Not only is playing poker a sin, it's a crime the way many people play it.

2. Playing cards is a pastime during which a good deal depends on just that.

3. Fact of life: It's amazing what great poker hands you get when you play bridge.

CAUTION

1. ~~The~~ There is only ~~thing you accomplish by~~ one problem with keeping your ear to the ground ~~is~~ that is, limiting your vision.

CENSORSHIP

1. Censors are people who stick their "nos" in other peoples' business.

CHAUVINISTS

See BACHELORS, FEMINISTS, GIGOLOS, MACHISMO, PLAYBOYS, FISHING 3

1. The problem with chauvinists is that they regard women as a passing fanny.

2. A chauvinist is a man who doesn't give women a second thought; the first one covered everything.

3. He's also someone who nags his wife about one undarned thing after another ...

4. ... and who believes he can marry any girl he pleases. Trouble is, he doesn't please any of them.

5. Actually, there are some women who would like to run into a chauvinist—when he's walking and they're driving.

6. A chauvinist is someone who makes dozens of women happy: He can only marry one of them.

CHEAPSKATES

See MONEY

1. A cheapskate is someone who earns their money the hoard way ...

2. ... whose motto is "Money doesn't grow on sprees" ...

3. ... who, when they go on a week's vacation, only spend seven days ...

4. ... who won't even sing a scale, since they hate parting with "doe."

5. And you have to hand it to them: Cheapskates always avoid picking up the check.

6. You might say a cheapskate is someone who's happy to let the rest of the world go buy ...

7. ... who doesn't care how he's treated, as long as he is ...

8. ... who's saving money for a rainy century ...

9. ... who marries a prostitute for her money ...

10. ... who not only pinches pennies but often pinches them from children.

11. When a cheapskate reaches for his wallet, George Washington has to shield his eyes from the light.

CHICKENS

See BIRDS, COMEDIANS 1

1. A chicken is the only animal you can eat before it's born and after it's dead.

2. Proud of their eggs, farmers have been known to boast "Better laid than ever!"

CHRISTMAS

See NEW YEAR'S EVE, THANKSGIVING

1. December 26 is the day we begin hearing the sound of Christmas bills.

2. Christmas is a time when Santa takes a day to deliver presents ... while we end up holding the bag the other 364.

3. It's also a day when people stay in to see how they came out.

4. Some people go to church once a year, on Christmas, and make weekly deposits in Christmas club accounts. Makes you wonder what they worship.

5. Christmas clubs are what keep you poor all year so that stores can be rich in December.

6. Jewelry is the best thing a man can buy a woman for the holidays: You can't go wrong ringing your Christmas belle.

7. All Christmas toys are educational: They teach children that their parents will buy almost anything.

8. Christmas is that magical time of year when all of your money disappears . . .

9. . . . when, unfortunately, there are fewer trees lit than people.

CLERGY

See RELIGION, MARRIAGE 9, THE TEN COMMANDMENTS 3

1. An evangelist is someone who takes the floor to hit the ceiling.

2. There was a time when the only little black book that belonged to a clergyman was the Bible.

3. Today, televangelists are people who need to have their faith lifted.

4. They're also people who take a big share of the pie out of piety.

5. In other words, to a televangelist, the only holy book is the checkbook.

6. Hoping to raise funds, the bishop ordered a contest between church choirs. The name? Battle of the Choral See.

CLOTHING *See* BATHING SUITS, BUSINESS 9,
GOLF 2, OLD AGE 19, SPEECHES 6,
STRIPPERS, 2, 5, 6, 7, 8, 9
TEENAGERS 8, WALLFLOWERS 2

1. The problem with too many secretaries is that they wear such tight dresses that the men in the office can hardly breathe.

2. Tight clothes don't stop a woman's circulation; in fact, they increase it.

3. With the price of clothes these days, it's cheaper to winter in the Bahamas than to buy an overcoat.

4. Of course, overcoats only last one season because they're designed to be worn out.

5. A sweater is a garment worn by a child when its mother feels cold.

6. A shoe store is one of the few places where they don't mind if the customer has a fit.

7. Perhaps furriers would do better if they didn't advertise for women to come in and be a miss in lynx.

8. Some men like a woman who shows style, but most prefer styles that show a woman.

COLLEGE

See SCHOOL, DENTISTS 3, HAIRDRESSERS 1, 2, LANGUAGE 3, NYMPHOMANIACS 10

1. Today, being college-bred means being a loaf for four years.

2. We've come a long way indeed from the time when women went to college simply to mate good.

3. In any college where there's a stacked student body, you're certain to find a faculty for love.

4. The problem with liberal arts schools is that they leave you well rounded but not pointed in any direction.

COMEDIANS

See JESTERS

1. A comedian is someone who does in a few
   seconds what it takes a chicken hours to
   accomplish.

COMMUNISM

See FREEDOM

1. In Communist countries, silence isn't golden;
   it's yellow.

2. Communist countries are those in which
   you have every right to speak your mind
   but no rights afterwards.

3. To put it another way, free speech isn't
   dead—only the speakers are.

4. Chernobyl proved that, in Russia, all men
   are cremated equal.

COMMUTERS

See PROGRESS 2

1. Why do they call it "rush hour" when traffic is at a standstill?

COMPLAINTS

1. If you don't have a leg to stand on, it's best not to kick.

CONCERTS

See COUNTRY SINGERS, MUSIC, ROCK STARS

1. A rap concert is a place where you go to mangle with the crowd.

CONSCIENCE

1. A conscience is something that hurts us when everything else feels terrific.

2. The reason most people have a clean conscience is that they never use it.

3. There may be more right-handed than left-handed people, but they're both outnumbered by the under-handed.

CONVERSATION

1. Why do they call it small talk, when there's so much more of it than any other kind?

COOKING

See DIETS, FOOD, RESTAURANTS, JAPS 2, 5

1. The great thing about cake mixes is that future generations will have no trouble making goodies just like mom used to make.

COUNTRY SINGERS

See CONCERTS,
MUSIC, ROCK STARS

1. A country singer is someone who uses two million dollars worth of equipment to sing about the simple life.

COWS

1. A cow is an animal that owes all it has to udders.

2. Milking a cow is the easiest thing in the world: Any jerk can do it.

3. As for bulls, old bulls never die, they just breed their last.

CREDIT CARDS

See MONEY,
CHRISTMAS 1, 2

1. A credit card is a way to increase your yearning capacity.

2. Credit cards are what's responsible for the mourning after.

3. Of course money can't buy everything. That's why there are credit cards.

4. An irony of modern life: More wallets would be fatter if they weren't filled with credit cards.

5. Credit cards are what make buying easy and paying hard ...

6. ... and what allow you to live within your budget and beyond your means.

7. Of course, go too much in debt and you'll find yourself discredited.

CRIME

See JUVENILE DELINQUENTS,
PLAGIARISM, PRISONS, MONEY 1,
MOTHERS-IN-LAW 4,
POLITICS 3, 4, 7, 8, 25, 26,
THE STOCK MARKET 3, 4, 7,
THE WORLD 1

BUSH

1. The problem with <u>too many neighbor</u>-hoods is that there <u>are more hoods than</u> neighbors.

2. Or, as aspiring burglars are learning, "If at first you don't succeed, try, try a gun."

3. People who lead checkered lives often end up in striped suits.

4. Old burglars never die, they just steal away.

5. A good pickpocket can remove your wallet with the skill of a surgeon ... though he won't make as much money.

CRITICS

See ACTORS 1

1. A theater critic is someone who stones the first cast.

CUSTOMS AGENTS

1. It's not that customs agents are crooked, but they *do* operate under the theory that what you seize is what you get.

DATING

See ENGAGEMENTS, PRUDES, SEX, BABIES 1, MARRIAGE 19, MOTION PICTURES 5, NYMPHOMANIACS 3

1. A girl on a date is like a typewriter: Press in the wrong place, and the words that come out are godawful.

2. A girl's nightmare: to be in a room with a handsome guy and have him ask her out.

3. A double negative makes a positive everywhere but on a date.

4. A blind date is when you pray for a vision but usually end up with a sight.

5. Unfortunately, most women are like movie serials: They stop just when you get to the interesting parts.

6. Alas, some women are so perfect that practice can't even make them.

7. It's a lucky man who finds a woman who likes to wash her hair, then neck.

8. A girl who looks like a dream usually ends up giving her date insomnia.

9. The best way to woo a woman with a past is with a present.

10. The problem with an old flame is that after she goes out a few times, she doesn't seem so hot.

11. When a man asks a girl up to see his etchings, it's usually not a standing invitation.

12. On a date, cooperation is when the woman coos and the man operates.

13. The reason so many women stay out late on dates is that men make them.

14. Many girls learn too late that soft soap can make them slip.

15. In short, a wise girl is the one who gets taken out, not taken in.

16. Though most girls can't be had for a song, many will respond to an overture.

17. Dating is a hit-or-miss proposition: A girl who doesn't make a hit remains a miss.

18. What most women look for in a beau is someone who's tall, dark, and has some . . .

19. . . . in other words, a man who's fiscally fit.

20. The worst thing that can happen to a man is to find a woman, paint the town red, then be given the brush.

21. Women claim that men are either so slow on dates they want to scream, or so fast they have to.

DEATH

See CAPITAL PUNISHMENT, BASTARDS 5, DISEASES 1, DOCTORS 4, FLOWERS 1, LOSERS 2, MOTHERS-IN-LAW 5

1. Most people agree that if you have to go, drowning in varnish provides the best finish.

2. Ever notice how everyone wants to go to heaven, but no one wants to die?

3. If you've got to kick the bucket, it's best to die with your boots on.

4. An unrecognized miracle: According to the newspapers, people today are dying in alphabetical order.

5. Not only is it true that you can't take it with you, but nowadays you can't even afford to go.

DENTISTS

See DOCTORS

1. If you argue with your dentist about pulling teeth, it usually ends in a draw.

2. The problem most of us have at the dentist's office is that we don't lose our nerve.

3. Dentistry is so popular today, you can't even get into school without the right kind of pull.

DIETS

See EXERCISE, FOOD, HEALTH, OBESITY

1. A diet is a weigh of life.

2. It's something most of us do religiously: We eat what we want and pray we don't gain weight.

3. A diet is what you go on when not only can't you fit into the store's dresses, you can't fit into the dressing room.

4. One guideline applies to fat and thin people alike: If you're thin, don't eat fast. If you're fat, don't eat ... fast.

5. The problem with curbing our appetites is that most of us do it at the drive-in window of McDonald's.

6. The most fattening thing you can put in an ice cream sundae is a spoon.

7. The biggest drawback to fasting for seven days is that it makes one weak.

8. Above all, dieters are advised to avoid Pepsi, the pause that refleshes.

9. Sweets are the destiny that shapes our ends.

10. Diets are for people who are thick and tired of it.

11. The toughest part of a diet isn't watching what you eat. It's watching what other people eat.

12. Diets are for women who not only kept their girlish figure but doubled it.

13. A diet is when you have to go to some length to change your width.

14. It's not the minutes spent at the table that put on weight, it's the seconds.

15. Many women reduce and reduce, yet still never manage to become a bargain.

16. The best way to lose weight is by skipping— snacks and desert.

17. Most people gain weight by having intimate dinners for two ... alone.

18. People go to Weight Watchers to learn their lessens.

19. A diet is the modern-day meal in which a family counts its calories instead of its blessings.

DIPLOMATS

See POLITICS

1. The worst diplomatic fate of all is to be a corrupt ambassador to China and to get yourself disoriented.

DISEASES

See AMNESIA, DOCTORS, HEALTH, HYPOCHONDRIACS, ULCERS, ALCOHOL 14, SEX 13, SPORTS 2

1. The most incurable disease For a is compulsive lying: Even after you're dead, you lie still.

2. The greatest drawback to being sick is that it leaves you in bed and bored.

3. Kleptomaniacs are people who help themselves because they can't help themselves.

4. The beauty of having a split personality is that when someone tells you to go screw yourself, you can oblige.

5. Indigestion is what you get when something you agreed with eats you.

DIVORCE

See ALIMONY, MARRIAGE, PALIMONY, SUCCESS 2

1. Today, if a man's wife looks like a new woman, chances are she is.

2. Nowadays, young lovers take one another for better or worse ... but rarely for good.

3. The mother who remembers her first kiss has a daughter who can't remember her first husband.

4. But nowadays, young women are extremely sentimental: They want to get divorced in the same dress their mother was divorced in.

5. According to most divorced couples, happiness is something that multiplies by division.

6. The problem with too many first mates is that they enjoy taking the wind from your sails.

7. The reason so many people divorce is that they forget that in wedding, the "we" comes before "i."

8. Another reason for divorce is when couples realize there was much " I do" about nothing.

9. In fact, "I do" is the only sentence that can be commuted for bad behavior.

10. Divorce is the result of a marriage that
    went from tense to past tense.

11. The problem with too many relationships
    is that they go from quest to conquest to
    inquest.

12. A divorce is a suit pressed with the seamy
    side out.

she'd been to only 4 weddings in her life... + they/we all were weddings

13. Modern lament: Always a bride, never a
    bridesmaid.

14. People who are off to be married elope.
    People who were off to be married divorce.
    off

15. Divorce might accurately be described as
    the longest mile of the wedding march.

16. Divorce comes from having popped the
    questioning before questioning the pop.

17. Divorce is the marital grave made from
    constant digging.

They ended in divorce/They tied the knot with

18. It's accurately referred to as the forget-me-
    knot.

DOCTORS   *See* DENTISTS, DISEASE, HEALTH,
NURSES, PHARMACISTS, PLASTIC
SURGERY, ALCOHOL 9, AMNESIA 2,
CRIME 5, HYPOCHONDRIACS 4,
OBESITY 6, OLD AGE 17,
SPECIALIZATION 2

1. If laughter were really the best medicine, doctors would have found a way to charge us for it.

2. Medical insurance is what allows people to be ill at ease.

3. A doctor is a person who enjoys bad health.

4. The reason optometrists live long lives is simple: They dilate.

5. Ever notice that while there are plenty of poor doctors, very few doctors are poor?

DOGS

See PETS, EMPLOYERS 13,
MARRIAGE 2, 18

1. Dogs are man's best friend because they wag their tails, not their tongues.

DRUNK DRIVERS *See* ALCOHOL, AUTOMOBILES

1. People who are driven to drink should always have a friend drive them back.

2. The problem with people who drink and drive is that after one too many, they take a turn for the worse.

3. It's a wise man who knows that when his cup runneth over, he should not runneth the car.

ECOLOGY

1. There was a time when a bad environment bred bad people. Now it's the other way around.

2. Nowadays, when guests drop over, it's usually due to radon.

3. In Los Angeles, the smog has gotten so bad that they're no longer fighting it, they're just putting Visine in fuel tanks.

4. Acid rain is made through a combination of sulfuric acid, nitric acid, and congressional apathy.

5. People who object to all the garbage washing up on beaches should swim when the ocean is tidy.

EGO

See FLATTERY, VANITY, YES-MEN, GOSSIP 13

1. People on ego trips should do others a favor and buy one-way tickets.

2. An egomaniac is someone who's hard of listening.

3. Blowing one's own horn only succeeds in deafening the listener.

4. You know someone has an ego problem when he joins the navy so the world can see him.

5. An egomaniac is someone who tells you his life story from A to Zzzzz.

6. The fact is, egomania is a form of I-dolatry ...

7. ... which leaves a person me-deep in any discussion.

8. Egomania is also known as a state of mine.

9. Egomaniacs are people who bring happiness whenever they go ...

10. ... who always open their mouth and put their feats in it.

11. People who're all wrapped up in themselves usually make pretty small packages.

12. An egomaniac is a self-made man who insists on giving everyone the recipe ...

13. ... who is mistaken in his belief that he can push himself forward by patting himself on the back ...

He told such tales about himself...

14. ... ~~who enters~~ *he enters* a room, dragging his tale behind him.

15. A swelled head is nature's attempt to fill a vacuum.

16. An egomaniac is someone who deprives you of privacy without providing any company ...

17. ... who not only holds a conversation, but strangles it.

18. There's this to be said for egomaniacs: The more you think of them, the less you think of them.

19. People who sing their own praises often find themselves performing a solo ...

... and usually out of tune.

EMBARRASSMENT

1. The best way to save face is to keep the bottom half shut. *or your face*

2. Another good way to save face is not to lose your head.

EMPLOYERS

See BASTARDS, BUSINESS, WORK, YES-MEN

1. A boss is a crank that turns the wheels of progress ...

2. ... who never loses his temper: It's always right there.

3. Why is it there's never enough time to do a job right, yet your boss always finds time for you to do it over?

4. A boss is someone who doesn't pull his own weight, just throws it around.

5. Ever notice that boss spelled backwards is double s-o-b?

6. An employer is someone who delegates all the authority, shifts all the blame, and takes all the credit.

7. Most bosses get where they are by the sweat of their browbeating . . .

8. . . . and by writing all their memos on wrapping paper.

9. Employers are people who have a lot of good in them. They must: it rarely comes out.

10. Employers are also people who were built all wrong—soft head, hard heart . . .

11. . . . who are people of rare good humor . . .

12. . . . who like to make employees crawl but usually get no further than the flesh.

13. Remember: To be top dog, you must first be a son of a bitch.

ENGAGEMENTS *See* DATING, HONEYMOONS, MARRIAGE, MARRIAGE LICENSES, WEDDINGS, PLAYBOYS 4

1. The thing most people do wrong is to get engaged at an early urge.

56

2. A marriage proposal is a proposition that got cold feet.

3. Most women won't play ball until a man provides the diamond.

4. The reason men aren't given engagement showers is that everyone knows they're washed up.

ESKIMOS

1. The Eskimos are fond of referring to themselves as "God's frozen."

2. The reason Eskimos don't wear armor is that there isn't enough armor: The knights are too damn long.

ETIQUETTE   *See* RESTAURANTS 1

1. Ever notice how many people eat with their fingers and talk with their fork?

EUPHEMISMS

1. In an effort to sound more macho, the Philosophy Debating Club has renamed itself Feud for Thought.

2. Trying to make "window shopping" sound a little less downscale, customers have taken to calling it "eye browsing."

EUROPE *See* PROGRESS 2, RESTAURANTS 2, 3, SEX 13

1. They got it wrong: Someone should have called them Parisites.

2. The reason it's called Ireland is that the inhabitants are always mad at someone.

3. Traveling anywhere in Europe is a hassle, but Helsinki is the worst: Your baggage vanishes into Finn Air.

EVOLUTION

See REDNECKS

1. We all sprang from the monkeys, but some people didn't spring far enough.

2. The problem with so many of us is that we're more concerned with what we're descended from than what we've descended to.

3. People who think we're the apex of creation have got it backwards. We're still just the ex-ape.

EXERCISE

See DIETS, HEALTH, OBESITY, GOLF 4, WEDDINGS 4

1. There is no workout more strenuous than having to push the thought of food to the back of your mind.

2. If God wanted JAPs to work out, he'd have put jewelry on the floor.

3. Exercise is what we do to loosen up, though most of us end up falling apart.

4. The problem with so many people who are musclebound is that they never get there.

5. Aerobics is a form of exercise invented to take our breadth away.

FAILURE

See BANKRUPTCY, LOSERS, SUCCESS, TROUBLE, THE STOCK MARKET 2, 8, 11, 13

1. Ever notice that the people who say, "That's the way the ball bounces" are usually the ones who dropped it?

2. Basically, failures are people with two faults: what they say and what they do.

FAME

1. The drawback of being the toast of the town is that all the people are trying to butter you up.

2. A celebrity is someone who works hard to become famous, then wears dark glasses to avoid being recognized.

3. A sure-fire way to get your name in the paper is to walk across the street reading one.

4. Too much celebrating has kept many people from becoming celebrated.

FEMINISTS   *See* CHAUVINISTS, WOMEN

1. Feminists are a paradox: They want to get ahead in the office, yet they resist advances.

2. Another paradox is the feminist who sits and deliberates.

3. Bad enough women always got the last word; now they add lib.

FISHING

1. Fishing is a pastime in which you have few bites but quite a few nips.

2. There are two kinds of fishers: those who fish for sport and those who catch something.

3. A man will sit on a boat all day, waiting for fish, then won't hesitate to complain if his dinner is a few minutes late.

FLATTERY
See EGO, YES-MEN

1. Flattery is telling others exactly what they think of themselves.

2. Flattery is fine, just as long as you don't inhale.

FLOWERS

See TREES, NYMPHOMANIACS 1

1. A dead flower is best described as a late bloomer.

2. The problem with creating a dried-flower arrangement is getting caught in the press. The result, alas, is a petrified florist.

3. Sadly, it's not possible to mix four-leaf clovers and poison ivy to get a rash of good luck.

4. Why is it that beautiful flowers die quickly, while blooming idiots are everywhere?

5. With the economy the way it is, the only growing concerns these days are flower shops.

FOOD

See COOKING, DIETS, OBESITY, RESTAURANTS, WINE, DISEASES 5, ETIQUETTE 1, FISHING 3, HEALTH 1, MARRIAGE, 4, THANKSGIVING 1

1. Indigestion is what you get when a square meal doesn't fit in a round stomach.

2. It's useless crying over spilled milk, unless it's condensed.

3. Of course there's no God: Why else would Swiss cheese have the holes when it's Limburger that needs the ventilation?

4. A cheese cake is something that turns to pound cake when you eat it.

5. People who don't go in the pool after a big meal would be better off trying the kitchen.

6. Forget the gas guzzler: The most expensive vehicle to operate, by the mile, is the shopping cart.

FOOTBALL   *See* BOXING, GOLF, SPORTS

1. A football stadium is where you pay cut-rate prices to see losing teams, and cutthroat prices to see winners.

2. Wise quarterbacks retire at their peak. The rest just pass away.

3. Worse, most over-the-hill quarterbacks spend their Sundays in the throws of agony.

4. Football is a game in which players go through four quarters and spectators through a fifth.

FREEDOM

See COMMUNISM,
THE UNITED STATES

1. A democratic country is one in which everyone has a right to state their opinions. And, luckily, no one is forced to listen.

2. A conservative believes that freedom is worth any price. And if you haven't got the money, you can't have it.

GAMBLING

See CARDS, LOTTERIES

1. The most important thing to remember about gambling is that money can be lost in more ways than one.

2. The problem with most gamblers is that when they start to go down, they refuse to abandon chips.

3. A race horse is an animal that can take thousands of people for a ride at the same time.

4. Strip poker is the one game in which the more you lose, the more you have to show for it.

5. In gambling, the surest way to end up with a small fortune is to start with a large one.

6. A compulsive gambler is someone who courts a rich woman so he can settle up.

7. A poker player is someone who frequently falls off his own bluff.

8. For gamblers, betting the rent money tends to be a moving experience.

9. The reason Las Vegas is so crowded is that no one has the plane fare to leave.

GENEALOGY

1. Anyone who spends a fortune to have their family tree researched is likely to find that they're the sap.

GIGOLOS
See BACHELORS, CHAUVINISTS, MACHISMO, PLAYBOYS, GAMBLING 6

1. A gigolo is a man who sells himself to the highest biddy ...

2. ... whose life is just a bed of ruses ...

3. ... who, when it comes to women, has what it takes to take what they have ...

4. ... to whom an act of love is just that.

GOLF
See BOXING, FOOTBALL, SPORTS, BUSINESS 3

1. The one time people *never* say, "It's just a game" is when they're winning.

2. It's a good idea for golfers to carry an extra pair of shoes, since they never know when they'll get a hole in one.

3. A fat man is someone who, if he puts the golf ball where he can hit it, can't see it; and if he puts it where he can see it, can't hit it.

4. A man who pushes a lawn mower and calls it work is the same man who pushes a golf cart and calls it recreation.

GOOD SAMARITANS

1. The problem today is that when it comes to doing good, most people stop at nothing.

GOSSIP See DOGS 1

1. Gossip is something that goes in one ear and in another.

2. Women who gossip are the spies of life.

3. A gossip is someone with a good sense of rumor . . .

4. . . . and who can't resist wordy causes.

5. The paradox about gossips is that they always talk about things that left them speechless.

6. What gossips hear is never as exciting as what they overhear.

7. A gossip's greatest fear is having no friends to speak of.

8. A gossip is someone who snares the unsuspecting in a mouth trap . . .

9. . . . whose train of thought runs people down . . .

10. . . . to whom a secret is either not worth keeping or too good to keep . . .

11. . . . who can give you all the details without knowing any of the facts . . .

12. . . . who compensates for a limited vocabulary with a large turnover.

13. Talk about others, and you're a gossip; talk about yourself, and you're a bore.

14. Gossips are people who never give secrets away; they trade them ...

15. ... who use dirt to make a mountain out of mole hill ...

16. ... who burn so much oxygen at the mouth, there's never any left for the brain ...

17. ... who don't mind their tongues, though everyone else does.

GUESTS

See ECOLOGY 2

1. Hospitality is making your guests feel at home, even when you wish they were.

2. Kindred, of course, is the fear that your relatives are coming.

3. With many guests, their shortcoming is their long-staying.

4. For most people, the worst kind of blood test is putting up with relatives.

HAIR

See HAIRDRESSERS, DATING 7, VANITY 3, 4

1. Some women are blonde on their mother's side, some on their father's side, but most on peroxide.

2. Many a dumb blonde is actually a smart brunette.

HAIRDRESSERS

See HAIR

1. A hairstylist's college is the only place you're rewarded for cutting class.

2. What's more, a hairdresser who fails is sure to be distressed.

HEALTH

See DIETS, DISEASES, EXERCISE, SMOKING, LANGUAGE 4, MISTRESSES 5, NUDISTS, 4, 5

1. Health food is something you nag your spouse to death to eat.

2. It may be true that men would live longer if they avoided drink, smoke, and women. But we'll never know until someone tries it.

3. Americans are getting fitter. Twenty years ago, it took two adults to carry fifty dollars' worth of groceries. Today, a child can do it.

4. A low-cholesterol diet is the key to heartening of the arteries.

5. A bed is where people who are run down wind up.

HIPPIES

1. Hippies were people who did their own thing because they didn't have a thing to do.

2. The reason the hippie movement finally died out is that they all became disjointed.

HONEYMOONS   *See* DATING, ENGAGEMENTS, MARRIAGE

1. You know your marriage is in trouble when your new bride is so tired she won't wake up for a second.

2. Once a woman's been carried over the threshold, she usually can't wait to put her foot down.

HORSES   *See* GAMBLING 3

1. There's nothing like horseback riding to make a person better off.

2. To put it another way, if you want to get what ails you off your mind, try riding a horse.

HYPOCHONDRIACS *See* DISEASES, DOCTORS, HEALTH

1. A depressed hypochondriac is someone who has no trouble to speak of.

2. Hypochondriacs are like people buying playoff tickets: Both have complaints of long-standing.

3. They're also like lady seers: both misfortunetellers.

4. Hypochondriacs are people who, when they wake up feeling well, call the doctor to find out what's wrong . . .

5. . . . and who exclaim "Good grief!" and mean it.

6. But the fact is that hypochondria is simply a case of sham pain.

INDECISION

1. The reason most people change their minds is that they never find one worth keeping.

INFIDELITY

See MISTRESSES, SEX

1. The difference between a wife and a mistress is night and day.

2. A philanderer is someone who has the two-time of his life.

3. A man who wants to pull the wool over his wife's eyes had better select the right yarn.

4. Unfaithful people are those who think that the plural of spouse is spice.

5. The wife of an adulterer usually won't speak to her husband for quite a time: the one he had with another woman.

6. A married man who's having an affair not only learns to dress well but quickly.

7. An unfaithful husband is one who takes his wife in a wedding dress, then gives her the slip.

8. A love triangle is a relationship that usually ends in a wreck-tangle.

9. According to researchers, the greatest cause of infidelity is a stalemate at home.

INFLATION

See MONEY, CLOTHING 3, HEALTH 3, PSYCHIATRISTS 3

1. Money still talks, only you have to turn up the volume to hear it.

2. Inflation is what transforms us from pushing a shopping cart into basket cases.

3. Today, it's easy to live in a more expensive apartment ... without even moving.

4. Inflation is so bad, you have to leave your VCR as a downpayment to get it fixed.

5. It's a sad day indeed when dollars to dough-
nuts is an even bet.

6. You know inflation is bad when it's the
leases that are breaking the tenants.

7. Inflation is so bad these days that money
doesn't *really* talk, it just goes without
saying.

INSURANCE

1. Buying insurance is what keeps people poor
so they can die rich.

INTELLIGENCE   *See* EGO 15, FLOWERS 4,
HAIR 2, INDECISION 1, MISTRESSES 3,
OLD AGE 20, POLITICS 18

1. Most people have minds like concrete: mixed
up or permanently set.

2. Other people have minds like blotters: They
soak everything in but get it all backwards.

3. When most people put in their two cent's worth, they aren't overcharging.

4. When something goes in one ear and out the other, it leaves a vacuum.

5. The reason things go in one ear and out the other is that there's nothing to block the traffic.

6. The problem with second opinions is that that's exactly how long most people think before offering them.

7. We would all benefit if we were surrounded by more open minds and fewer open mouths.

8. The mind is like a television: When it goes blank, it's a good idea to turn off the sound.

9. The problem with jumping to conclusions is that there's never a safety net.

10. The reason talk is cheap is that the supply far outpaces the demand.

11. The trouble with most people is that they have diarrhea of the mouth but constipation of the brain.

12. Ever notice that the people who give you a piece of their minds are usually the ones who can least afford to?

13. The only reason some people are lost in thought is that they're total strangers there.

14. It's safe to call such people decaffeinated: There's nothing active in the bean.

15. If most people said what's on their minds, they'd be speechless.

16. People who speak straight from the shoulder rarely tap anything higher up.

17. The problem with most people who reach their wits' end is that it doesn't take them long to get there.

18. The problem today is that there are fewer people with open minds and more with holes in their heads.

19. Today, when most people offer sound advice, it's 99 percent sound and 1 percent advice.

20. In fact, the most unexpected injury most people suffer nowadays is being struck by an idea.

21. Some people are so dumb, driving them out of their minds is overkill: All it takes is a short putt.

22. The problem with most people's brainchildren is they're stillborn.

23. If ignorance is bliss, why aren't more people happy?

24. Most people are like rivers: There's usually more activity at the mouth than at the source.

25. Air is matter that has little substance and, when it comes from most peoples' mouth, has even less.

26. Some people get up bright and early; most people just get up early.

27. Most people don't act stupid; it's the real thing.

28. They're called "pearls of wisdom" because, where most people are concerned, they're so rare.

29. Most folks stop to think. The trouble is, they forget to start again.

INVENTORS

1. An inventor is a crackpot who becomes a genius when his ideas catch on.

2. Inventors are also people who can make everything ... except a living.

JAPS   *See* EXERCISE 2

1. A JAP is a woman who sweeps the room with a glance ...

2. ... who can dish it out, but can't cook it ...

3. ... who's extremely gifted and has three closets to keep it all in ...

4. ... who sticks by a man with a will of his own, as long as she's the beneficiary ...

5. ... for whom c--kbook is a dirty word; that's *cookbook*, not *checkbook*.

6. A JAP's idea of a romantic setting is one that has a diamond in it.

7. A JAP is someone who's always letting the cattiness out of the bag ...

8. ... who not only walks all over her husband but does it with spiked heels ...

9. ... who takes a painkiller ... and dies.

JESTERS

See COMEDIANS

1. An out-of-work jester is nobody's fool.

JUDGES

See LAWYERS

1. A judge is an attorney who's stopped practicing law.

2. And is there anything more disgraceful than a judge who is disappointed ... or, worse, dishonored?

JUVENILE DELINQUENTS

See CRIME

1. Most juvenile delinquents are kids who go from being unwanted to being wanted.

2. A bold juvenile delinquent is one who murders his parents, then asks for clemency on the grounds he's an orphan.

3. A *real* juvenile delinquent is one who goes to reform school ... on a scholarship.

KIDS

1. Children are imps who cause parents to feel old and grandparents to feel young.

2. A child is someone who knows all the questions at age eight, and all the answers at age eighteen.

3. Children who are raised in tents only grow to a point

4. The problem with most parents today is that they give their kids a free hand ... but not in the right place.

5. In fact, the best thing for a kid who spends too much time sowing his wild oats is a good thrashing.

6. A brat is a kid whose training didn't begin at the bottom ...

7. ... and who would be smarter upstairs if he smarted downstairs.

8. Parents who put their foot down will find their kids reluctant to step on their toes.

9. To put it another way, more kids would be better off if doting parents were *don'ting* parents.

10. In general, kids are what make parents want to jump for joy ... off very tall buildings.

11. You might say that having children is a fetal mistake.

12. Sex must be a sin. Look how parents are punished for it.

13. The truth is, children are more difficult to bear after birth than before.

14. You might say that children should be seen and not had.

15. You can always tell a mother on the brink: She shoots her husband with a bow and arrow so she won't wake the kids.

16. Kids may not always succeed, but most of the time parents find them trying.

17. A parent is someone who begets children, bores teenagers, and boards newlyweds.

18. Nowadays, the accent may be on youth, but the stress is on their parents.

19. Parents are never more content than when their children are in bed, safe and soundless.

LANGUAGE

1. English is a language in which double negatives are a no-no ...

2. ... in which a fat chance and a slim chance mean the same thing ...

3. ... in which the term "mental institution" can be used to describe an asylum or a college ...

4. ... in which a Mr. Universe and a couch potato can earn the same reward: atrophy ...

5. ... in which just one letter makes all the difference between here and there ...

6. ... in which "hi" and "lo" have the same meaning.

7. The good thing about mincing your words is that they're easier to eat later on.

8. Sad but true: Why bother speaking correct English? No one will understand you.

9. Only in English can day break when it's night that falls.

LAWYERS   *See* JUDGES

1. Talk is cheap, but only if lawyers aren't doing the talking.

2. An attorney is a person who'll read a forty-page document and call it a brief.

3. But a lawyer's lawyer is someone who names his daughter Sue.

LITERATURE

See CENSORSHIP, ART 3, BUSINESS 5

1. The problem with reading the Cliff Notes version of *Walden* is that it's not very Thoreau.

2. Always remember: No matter how much you hate reading prose, it could be verse.

3. Most contemporary writing deserves the Pulitzer Prize—or at least the first two letters.

LOSERS

See FAILURE, TROUBLE

1. A loser is someone who gives his girl friend a gift certificate and she exchanges it ...

2. ... who was poor all his life, and upon whose death the gravediggers strike oil ...

3. ... who wasn't wicked enough to enjoy this life but wasn't good enough to enjoy the next.

LOTTERIES   *See* GAMBLING, MONEY

1. You can count on it: When your ship finally comes in, you'll find friends and relatives waiting at the dock.

2. They call them breadwinners, because the only way a family can afford to eat is if they win the lottery.

LOVE   *See* GIGOLOS 4, MARRIAGE 18, 20, NYMPHOMANIACS 8, SCHOOL 5

1. Love is like a bag of groceries: The more you put into it, the heavier it gets.

2. Love is something that evolves over the years: It goes from her sinking into his arms with joy to her arms in a sink with Joy.

3. Ever notice that while love is sometimes just infatuation, hate is always the real thing?

4. Love is a word consisting of two vowels, two consonants, and two fools.

5. Love is a condition in which a woman without any sense marries a man without any money.

LUCK
See FLOWERS 3

1. The problem with relying on luck is that while you're outside looking for four-leaf clovers, you may miss opportunity knocking.

opportunity is diguised as hardwood

MACHISMO
See BACHELORS, CHAUVINISTS, GIGOLOS, PLAYBOYS, REDNECKS, EUPHEMISM 1

1. Ever notice that hard-boiled eggs are yellow inside?

2. A macho-man is one that women find difficult to resist; in fact, they have to fight him off.

3. A macho-man is also someone whose comeons turn a girl's stomach, not her head.

4. In fact, the only way those lines will get him anywhere is if he puts a sail in front of his mouth.

5. Sadly, he also believes that all women like to be taken with a grain of assault.

MAIDS

1. Many a woman has had to let the maid go because her husband wouldn't.

MARRIAGE   *See* DATING, DIVORCE,
ENGAGEMENTS, HONEYMOONS,
INFIDELITY, LOVE, MARRIAGE LICENSES,
MOTHERS-IN-LAW, WEDDINGS,
ALCOHOL 18, CHAUVINISTS 4, 6,
CHEAPSKATES 9, COLLEGE 2,
JAPS 8, MAIDS 1, TRAVEL 6,
WALLFLOWERS 4

1. A husband who married his secretary is a man who now takes dictation.

2. You know you've been married too long when it's the dog who brings you the paper and your wife who barks.

3. Marriage is like a bath: Once you've been in it a while, it's not so hot.

4. It's also like eating a mushroom: By the time you find out it's bad, it's too late.

5. In short, marriage isn't a word, it's a sentence.

6. You know a man is henpecked when the champagne bottles in his home all go "mom."

7. Marriage is a three-ring circus: engagement ring, wedding ring, suffering.

8. Marriage may be a blessed union, but wait until you start paying those union dues.

9. Speaking of which, the clergy are people who collect those union "I dos."

10. Whoever said "talk is cheap" never said "I do."

11. Many young women take older men to the cleaners the instant they spot them.

12. A shotgun wedding is a case of wife or death.

13. Cardplaying is not the only expensive undertaking that begins with holding a hand.

14. A husband is a man who started by handing out a line and ended up toeing one.

15. Marriage is like a meal in which the dessert is the first course.

16. A husband is a diplomat who remembers his wife's birthday but not her age ...

17. ... who pays no attention to his wife but gets jealous when someone else does.

18. The problem with so many marriages is that what starts out as puppy love often goes to the dogs.

19. Marriage is when dating gives way to intimidating ...

20. ... when you go from swearing to love to loving to swear.

MARRIAGE LICENSES   See ENGAGEMENT, MARRIAGE

1. A marriage license is a hunting license for one dear only.

2. And doesn't it figure? It's the only license that never expires.

THE MILITARY

See EGO 4

1. If you think old soldiers fade away, you should watch one trying to get into an old uniform.

2. The navy is what you join to see the world ... and then spend two years in a submarine.

MISTRESSES

See INFIDELITY, WOMEN 11

1. A mistress is someone who lives in a beautiful apartment until her louse expires ...

2. ... who, despite her talents, has maintained her amateur standing ...

3. ... who is often so dumb she can't count on her fingers, though she can always count on her hips and chest.

4. The trouble with mistresses is that they're looking for a husband instead of a single man.

5. A little honey is good for a man's health, unless his wife finds out.

MOBILE HOMES

1. The problem with mobile homes is parking them on a hill: They can leave if they're so inclined.

MONEY

1. Nowadays, people are so poor that when burglars break into houses, all they get is practice.

2. Today, the only thing you can count on as being free of charge is a day-old battery.

3. In the old days, the man of the house was called "papa"; today, he's called "pauper."

4. You can tell the economy is fit: Look how fast money goes.

5. You can try paying your debts with a smile, but they'll still want money.

6. The reason the economy is bouncing back is because so many checks are made of rubber.

7. It's called "cold cash" because it's never in your pocket long enough to get warm.

8. Saving is when people skimp on what they need to buy what they can live without.

9. Money is called legal tender because when you don't have it, it's rough.

10. The only time you can count on people to be good listeners is when money talks.

11. A deficit is what you have when you haven't as much as you did when you had nothing.

12. The problem with spending money like water is that you'll have trouble floating a loan.

13. As a last resort to debt, there's always the IOU, also known as a paper wait.

14. With the economy so weak, the only business in which you can be sure to make a mint is the candy business.

15. Nowadays, most young people have the same goal: to make a little money first, then make a little money last.

16. Money talks ... but just to say good-bye.

17. Actually, with prices the way they are these days, money just stutters.

18. Nowadays, the economy is truly electrical: Everything is charged.

19. It's called take-home pay, because there's nowhere else you can go with it.

20. The good news is that the dollar will never fall as low as the means some people use to get it.

21. The bottom line is that saving your money is a good idea. Some day, it may be worth something again.

MOTELS

1. A motel is where you stop to take a road off your mind.

MOTHERS-IN-LAW

1. A mother-in-law is someone who belongs to the meddle class.

2. Ever notice that a husband talks about his mother-in-law as if his wife didn't have one?

3. The man who claims that his mother-in-law can't take a joke forgets himself.

4. The real penalty for bigamy is having two mothers-in-law.

5. Most men would jump at the chance to smother their mother-in-law with diamonds. It'd be worth the expense.

6. A mother-in-law is someone who knocks on your door ... and then everything else in sight ...

7. ... someone who is never, ever outspoken ...

8. ... who is no laughing matter ...

9. ... who thinks the man who wasn't good enough to marry her daughter has fathered the brightest grandchild on earth.

MOTION PICTURES   See ACTORS, CRITICS, FAME, DATING 5

1. In many places, people worship the cross. In Hollywood, that goes double.

2. An art house is a theater in which the aisles are clean and the film is dirty.

3. In fact, *all* of Hollywood has degenerated into a place where they put beautiful frames in filthy pictures.

4. Hollywood would be much improved if they shot fewer films and more filmmakers.

5. Many people mourn the death of the drive-in, better known as a place with wall-to-wall car-petting.

MOTORCYCLE *See* AUTOMOBILES

1. Motorcyclists who bike without helmets should get their heads examined ... and usually do.

MUSIC *See* CONCERTS, COUNTRY SINGERS, OPERA, ROCK STARS, ALCOHOL 15, CHEAPSKATES 4, CLERGY 6, DATING 16

1. A bad musician is someone who should keep his dissonance.

NEW YEAR'S EVE

See CHRISTMAS,
THANKSGIVING

1. December 31 is a day when old friends try not to pass out before the old year.

2. On New Year's Eve, we have countless resolutions; on New Year's Day, we learn we have none.

NUDISTS

1. Nudists are people who are wrapped up only in themselves.

2. It's not surprising that nudists don't always get along: They see too much of each other.

3. A nudist colony is the only place where you communicate by barely talking . . .

4. . . . where there are incredible athletes: Everyone there runs the fifty-yard dash in nothing . . .

5. ... which is a good thing: They'd be thrown out if they stopped for short pants.

6. There's nothing wrong with being a nudist: All of us are born that way.

NURSES   *See* DOCTORS

1. Most nurses are young women who hold your wrist and then expect your pulse to be normal.

NYMPHOMANIACS   *See* SEX, DATING 9

1. A nymphomaniac is like a flower: She grows wild in the woods.

2. She's someone who can go lap after lap without tiring ...

3. ... who lives from date to date ...

4. ... who advances pulses instead of repulsing advances ...

5. ... and who, before she goes to bed, offers a heartfelt "Ah, men!"

6. She's the kind of girl who, if Moses had known her, there would have been another Commandment ...

7. ... who doesn't enjoy going out to do things but in to undo things ...

8. ... who is glad that love is blind, so that men have to feel their way around.

9. She's a woman whose won'ts are few ...

10. ... who, in college, wore a sweater with a letter because she'd made the team ...

11. ... whose body language speaks volumes, though it's far from being a first edition ...

12. ... and who enjoys sitting in a bar and watching the men come buy.

13. In the final analysis, a nymphomaniac is a woman, after all.

OBESITY

See DIET, EXERCISE, FOOD, HEALTH, GOLF 3, TRAVEL 3, WOMEN 8

1. Say what you want, fat men have what it takes to attract women: gravity.

2. As for a fat woman, she isn't a sight; she's a panorama.

3. To an obese person, a well-balanced diet is a pizza in each hand.

4. Middle age is an age when most people grow in the middle.

5. Women become fat from eating too much: They hear that food becomes them, and they misunderstand.

6. On the other hand, many people diet when told to by their doctors. After all, a word to the wide is sufficient.

7. Unfortunately for most people, overeating ends up being a big waist of time.

OLD AGE

See BIRTHDAYS, DEATH, RETIREMENT, SEX 4, STRIPPERS 4, WINE 1, WOMEN 16, 22

1. The biggest thing wrong with the young generation is that most of us aren't part of it anymore.

2. One thing you realize during an uphill struggle is how fast you're going downhill.

3. The only thing that becomes easier as you grow older is getting tired.

4. Sadly, when you learn to make the most of life, most of life is gone ...

5. ... but it's better to be old and bent than old and broke.

6. Those who say their age is their own business have usually been in business for a long time.

7. The problem with dirty old men is that they may be hungry for young girls, but young girls are too hungry for them.

8. You know you're getting old when you turn out the bedroom light to lower the electric bill instead of a woman's nightie.

9. Another sure sign of age is when you admire the dish at the restaurant, instead of the dish who brought it.

10. The problem with old age is that now that you know your way around, you don't feel like going.

11. Old age is when it takes longer to rest than it did to get tired ...

12. ... when you feel like the day after when it's the day before ...

13. ... and when you have thoughts about women, instead of feelings.

14. A woman can fake youth by using a good mascara to bring out her eyes and a good lipstick to bring out her lips ... until a good sneeze brings out her teeth.

15. There's nothing more pathetic than an old goat trying to act like a kid ...

16. ... unless it's an elderly man trying to get to first base with an old bat.

17. Old age is when all the phone numbers in your little black book belong to doctors.

18. Alas, by the time a man can read a woman like a book, he's too old to start a library.

19. A woman knows she's getting old when she worries more about how her shoes fit than how her sweater fits.

20. People are only as old as they think. That makes most of them about two.

OPERA *See* MUSIC

1. The opera is a place where a man is stabbed and, instead of bleeding, he sings ...

2. ... and where something that sounds stupid when spoken sounds fine when sung.

OPTIMISTS

See PESSIMISTS

1. Optimists are people who get wealthy by buying out pessimists.

2. An optimist invented the boat; a pessimist invented the life preserver.

PALIMONY

See DIVORCE, WOMEN 20

1. Palimony is when a woman doesn't take a broken relationship to heart, but to court.

2. It's a suit men get from chasing a skirt.

PERFUME

1. Perfume is what a woman hopes will make her the scenter of attraction.

2. Perfume manufacturers are people who stick their business in other people's noses.

PESSIMISTS

See OPTIMISTS

1. A pessimist is someone who looks at life through morose-colored glasses ...

2. ... who break mirrors, just to make sure they live another seven years ...

3. ... and who burn all their bridges ahead of them.

PETS

See DOGS

1. The problem with this generation is that people are trading in dogs and cats for pet peeves.

PHARMACISTS

See DOCTORS

1. Nowadays, a pharmacist is someone who puts on a white coat, stands behind a soda fountain, and sells batteries.

PHILANTHROPY

See SUCCESS

1. Philanthropists are people who steal privately so they can give publicly.

PLAGIARISM

1. A plagiarist is someone who coins a phrase that proves to be counterfeit.

PLASTIC SURGERY

See DOCTORS, VANITY

1. A facelift is something that takes care of a multitude of skins.

PLAYBOYS

See BACHELORS, DATING, CHAUVINISTS, GIGOLOS, MACHISMO

1. A playboy is a broad-minded man ...

2. ... someone who has the angles if a woman has the curves ...

3. ... who treats all women as sequels.

4. At best a playboy is a passing fiance ...

5. ... someone who's tall, dark, and hands.

6. A playboy is someone who believes that sleep is the best thing there is ... next to a woman ...

7. ... who men don't trust very far, and women don't trust very near.

PLANETARIUMS

1. A planetarium is not only a show with a cast of thousands, but every one's a star.

PLUMBERS

1. Only when the plumbing's stopped up do you realize that a flush is better than a full house.

POLITICAL CONVENTIONS   *See* POLITICS

1. A political convention is where the parties put their best fool forward.

POLITICS

See DIPLOMATS, POLITICAL
CONVENTIONS, ECOLOGY 4,
SPEECHES 7, 8

1. In politics, after all is said and done, a lot more is said than done.

2. The problem with politicians who have little to say is that you have to listen to so much to find that out.

3. The reason politicians are so busy is that the time they don't spend passing laws, they spend helping friends get around them.

4. And the reason our form of government has so much support is that so many politicians are holding it up.

5. Political speeches are a lot like cattle horns: There are a few good points but a lot of bull in the middle.

6. The only difference between a politician and a speck of dirt is that the politician usually manages to stay in the public eye without irritating it.

7. Influence peddlers are people who, more and more, are becoming the lifers of the party.

8. Today, when politicians tell voters "I've never taken a bribe, give me a chance," they mean just that.

9. The dilemma facing a woman in politics is simple: If she's bad-looking, the men won't vote for her. And if she's good-looking, the women won't.

10. Today, the only time you can be sure a politician is telling the truth is when he calls another politician a liar.

11. Elections are when people find out what a politician stands for and politicians find out what people will fall for.

12. The problem with the vast halls of Congress is that they're filled with half-vast politicians.

13. Governor Dukakis mistakenly believed he was a shoo-in because he had Mass appeal.

14. The good thing about money is that not only does it talk, but in the right hands it stops talk.

15. Being an intelligent and fair politician wins the votes of thinking people. Unfortunately, election requires a majority.

16. A politician is someone who's full of promises.

17. Some politicians are good; some are lousy. That makes the breed good and lousy.

18. A politician is someone who gets a good idea only when he's out of his mind.

19. The reason most politicians stand on their records is that so voters can't get a look at them.

20. Most politicians succeed by passing the buck ... and dough.

21. An honest politician is like the earth: Both are flattened at the polls.

22. Nowadays, politicians are more ambitious than ever: Not only are they leaders of men, they're followers of women.

23. They're also people skilled at mending fences with hedging.

24. A politician is someone who has a perfect grasp of the questions of the day but doesn't know any of the answers.

25. A politician is, quite frankly, the best person money can buy.

26. The reason politicians want to kick the crooks out of government is that they can't stand the competition.

27. An honest politician is someone who quickly gets seasick on the ship of state.

THE POST OFFICE

1. If the world keeps shrinking, why do postal rates keep rising?

2. A philatelist is a dummy who pays more for used stamps than for new ones.

3. Letter-writers are magicians who can pen moving letters on stationery paper.

PRISONS
See CAPITAL PUNISHMENT, CRIME, JUVENILE DELINQUENTS

1. Prisons are places people go to in a pinch.

2. As for prisoners, they're best described as birds in guilt cages.

3. Crime should not be cured in the electric chair. It should be cured in the high chair.

PROGRESS

1. People have been able to improve on everything but people.

2. Progress is when it takes shorter and shorter to get to Europe and longer and longer to get to work.

3. Progress is finding yourself watching *Tora! Tora! Tora!* on your Sony TV.

PROSTITUTES   *See* CHEAPSKATES 9

1. A prostitute is a woman with a great figure that men try to meet.

2. Most prostitutes find that a nice smile adds to their face value.

3. Of course, nothing quite defines "waste" better than a smile sitting atop a forty-inch bust.

4. Prostitutes have also learned that falsies are helpful as a cure for absentease.

5. A down-and-out hooker is one who can't get back on her back.

6. A whore is a woman who has been tried and found wanton ...

7. ... whose success is measured in man-hours ...

8. ... who's good for nothing, but never bad for nothing ...

9. ... who is never free for the night.

10. The difference between a career woman and a prostitute is that one moves ahead, the other a behind.

11. A madam is someone for whom the belles toil.

12. Many hookers could be cured of their ways if they'd see a shrink. But it galls them to lie on a man's couch and pay him.

PRUDES *See* WALLFLOWERS, DATING 1, 3, 6

1. A prude is someone who whispers sweet nothing-doings in your ear.

PSYCHIATRISTS *See* DISEASES 4, PROSTITUTES 12, SWEARING 2

1. A thoughtful analyst is one who gets a sectional couch for his patients with split personalities.

2. An opportunistic analyst is one who charges that same patient $100 an hour . . . each.

3. Psychiatry is an expensive proposition: Nowadays, all you get for $50 is a get-well card.

4. In fact, for most patients, psychiatrists don't resort to traditional shock treatment. They simply present the bill up-front.

5. Psychiatrists are people who take you in when you're slightly cracked and leave you totally busted.

6. The irony of psychiatry is that you have to lie down to learn how to stand on your own two feet.

7. Some psychiatrists are so strict they give their patients homework: they send them straight home to dream.

8. As far as shrinks are concerned, when it comes to sanity, most people have an in.

9. The problem with most paranoiacs is that they're self-taut.

10. A psychiatrist catering exclusively to egomaniacs describes her practice as "a site for sore I's."

RADIO

See TELEVISION

1. A disc jockey is someone who works for the love of mike.

REDNECKS

See MACHISMO

1. Rednecks may not be the missing links in evolution, but they're certainly the weakest links.

RELIGION

See CLERGY, THE TEN COMMANDMENTS

1. An atheist is someone with no invisible means of support.

2. Worship is insurance we take out in this life against a fire in the next.

3. A long as there are math tests, there will always be prayer in school.

RESTAURANTS

See COOKING, FOOD, CHEAPSKATES 5, 6, 7, OLD AGE 9

1. The trouble with eating out is that the tables are reserved, but the diners aren't.

2. One thing to remember when eating in a German restaurant: No matter how bad the appetizer is, the wurst is yet to come ...

3. ... but the good news is that you'll always be with the "in kraut."

4. A restaurant is a place in which, the tenderer the meat, the tougher it is to swallow the check.

5. Overly chic is the Chinese restaurant that prints its menu in French.

6. Nowadays, an after-dinner mint is what people need to pay their restaurant tab.

7. A restaurant is the only place where people are happy when they're fed up.

RETIREMENT   *See* OLD AGE

1. Retirement is when you finally have the time to sink your teeth into something fun ... but you don't have the teeth.

ROCK STARS

See CONCERTS, COUNTRY SINGERS, MUSIC

1. In the old days, singers had a two-C range: high C and low C. Today, they have just one: louse C.

2. Music comes out easy for most rock singers. No wonder: They flatten the notes.

3. The problem with so many rock singers is that they know the secret of good music . . . and keep it to themselves.

4. All rock musicians have this in common with Horowitz, Casals, and Heifetz: They play with both hands.

5. Most rock singers are people who, when they try to carry a tune, buckle under the load.

6. A rock and roller is someone who can't help singing—by doing it.

SALESPEOPLE

See BUSINESS

1. A good salesperson is one who makes a living going door to door selling signs that read, "No salespeople allowed."

2. The trouble with being a door-to-door hearing-aid salesperson is that your best prospects never answer.

3. Humans are the only animals that can be skinned more than once.

SCHOOL

See COLLEGE, RELIGION 3, SPORTS 1

1. The problem with being voted most popular in school is that the other kids hate you for it.

2. A teacher is someone who bores without striking oil.

3. The problem with students who spend half their time making jokes is that they end up as half-wits.

4. An answer no teacher will mark wrong: The most powerful nation on earth is determination.

5. The problem with students who fall in love with their teachers is that they put the heart before the course.

6. A teacher is someone who talks in other peoples' sleep.

SEX *See* BIRTH CONTROL, DATES, INFIDELITY, MISTRESSES, NYMPHOMANIACS, PLAYBOYS, PROSTITUTES, BABIES 5, CLERGY 2, COLLEGE 3, KIDS 12, MAIDS 1, OLD AGE 7, 8, 13, POLITICS 22, WOMEN 11, 12, 14

1. A woman's face may be her fortune, but it's the other parts that attract the most interest.

2. The problem with women who are built like a brick outhouse is that they rarely get plastered.

3. You can tell a woman's frigid when the circles under her eyes are Arctic.

4. Sex is something that evolves over the years from triweekly to try weekly to try weakly.

5. ~~Men~~ aren't led into temptation. They find it all by themselves.

6. The truth is, most people aren't troubled by improper thoughts; they enjoy them.

7. The problem with bathing beauties is that most of us never get to.

8. Infants don't have nearly as much fun in infancy as adults have in adultery.

9. Lovers' lane is where men retreat to make advances.

10. A kiss is an application for a better position.

11. Men with money to burn have started many women playing with fire.

12. While it's true that some women can attract men with their mind, more attract men with what they don't mind.

13. In Scandinavia, free love is practiced. It's the penicillin that costs.

SKATING

1. The problem with most skaters is that they do it for hours on end.

2. Not only that, but everyone jokes when you fall. Even the ice makes cracks.

SMOKING   *See* HEALTH 2

1. Smokers are people who puff on cigarettes, cigars, and steps.

SPECIALIZATION

1. Specialists are people who know more and more about less and less.

2. In this era of specialization, what four out of five doctors end up recommending is another doctor.

SPEECHES
See POLITICS 2, 5

1. A good speech consists of a good beginning and a good ending ... preferably, close together.

2. Many speakers need no introduction, just a conclusion.

3. Too many speakers claim to be speaking for posterity. Unfortunately, they're so long-winded posterity gets to hear it first-hand.

4. Some speakers need to put fire into their speeches; others, just the opposite.

5. When listening to speakers, one is often forced to wonder who writes their immaterial.

6. A speech should be like a woman's skirt: long enough to cover the subject, but short enough to generate interest.

7. Most politicians don't bore people with long speeches. They do it with short ones.

8. Election is a time when there are speeches in the air, and vice versa.

SPORTS   *See* BOXING, FISHING, FOOTBALL, GOLF, SKATING

1. You know that schools are overemphasizing sports when students think the three "Rs" are "rah, rah, rah!"

2. More often than not, athlete's foot comes from an athlete's feat.

1. In the past, stocks split. Today, they just fall apart.

2. Fortunately, most people weren't ruined by the crash of '87. They went broke in '86.

3. The problem with so many stock brokers these days is that they carve out their careers by chiseling.

The crooked Wall Street broker + g sculpter have in common

4. Stock brokers are people who move in the right circles, which is why they rarely go straight.

5. Things are so bad these days that seats on the stock exchange come equipped with seat belts.

6. Today, the smartest animal on Wall Street isn't the bull or bear, it's the chicken.

7. Most traders today play the market dictionary style: Invest is followed by investigation.

8. When the stock market falls, millions lose their balance.

9. Nowadays, the only time investors make killings in the stock market is when they shoot their brokers.

10. People who put money in the stock market usually don't have money to put in the supermarket.

11. In the old days, it was the laundry that called and said it had lost your shirt. Today, it's your stock broker.

12. Though the laundry and the stock exchange might as well merge: Go to either, and you're taken to the cleaners.

13. Which is why they call them "brokers." When you deal with them, that's what you become.

1. Strippers are most successful when there's a call for their re-peel.

2. You might say they're people who get the most out of their costumes.

3. On the other hand, nothing is quite so pathetic as a stripper who is all undressed with no place to show.

4. In general, strippers are people who use what Mother Nature gave them before Father Time takes it away.

5. Fact: Whatever you give a stripper to wear, her heart usually isn't in it.

6. She usually wears unmentionables—that is, nothing to speak of.

7. When they *do* choose their clothing, though, strippers dress to be seen in the best places.

8. You might say, in fact, that when they dress, they go all out.

9. Of course, their wardrobe is designed not to make them look good, but to make men look good.

10. Fortunately, there's always hope for strippers: Each morning is the dawn of a nude day.

11. In the final analysis, a woman of this sort is simply someone who's trying to outstrip her competition.

12. Or, as one pundit put it, she's a woman in her salad days ... without the dressing.

SUCCESS

See FAILURE, PHILANTHROPY, WEALTH, EGO 12, 13, OPTIMISTS 1, PROSTITUTES 7, SALESPEOPLE 1, SCHOOL 4

1. The only difference between a stumbling block and a stepping stone is the way you use it.

2. A man generally owes success to his first wife and his second wife to success.

3. Too many people believe that the best w[ay]
   up the ladder of success is to kiss the feet
   of those above them, and step on anyone
   below them.

SUMMERTIME

1. Summer is when you sit in traffic to sit at
   the beach ...

2. ... when your kids slam the doors they left
   open all winter ...

3. ... when you try to make your house as
   cold as you complained it was during the
   winter.

SUPERSTITION

1. Superstitions are little more than myth-beliefs.

SWEARING

See DATING 1, MARRIAGE 20, TAXES 3, WOMEN 9

1. Nowadays, people are so vituperative that one four-letter word per sentence is par for the coarse.

2. A woman whose son won't stop swearing is sure to find a shrink willing to discuss him.

Cursing → w/ a vengence
vs.
Cussing → w/ a heart

TABLOIDS

1. A tabloid reporter is one who can smell a juicy story a mile away. After it's written, so can the readers.

TAXES

See INFLATION, MONEY

1. April 15 is the only day when blanks can kill.

2. According to the government, a taxpayer is someone who has what it takes.

3. The IRS is a place that says, "Watch your step" going in, and "Watch your language" going out.

4. The ideal situation, of course, is for the government to live within its means and without yours.

5. The IRS is a pain in the neck, and some people have an even lower opinion of them.

6. People who save their money for a rainy day end up getting soaked by the government.

7. Taxation is a bizarre system in which you spend money, save receipts, and somehow come out ahead.

TEENAGERS *See* BABIES, KIDS, AUTOMOBILES 5

1. A teenager is a girl who puts lipstick on, and a boy who wipes it off.

2. When teenagers want to drive, wise parents don't stand in their way.

3. Teenagers are people who get ten hours of sleep a day, and none of it at night ...

4. ... who stop asking where they came from and won't tell you where they're going ...

5. ... who are human gimme-pigs ...

6. ... who are alike in so many disrespects ...

7. ... who want for nothing ...

8. ... who express their desire to be different by dressing alike ...

9. ... and who are at that awkward age: They know how to start a phone call but not how to end it.

TELEVISION

See RADIO, INTELLIGENCE 8, PROGRESS 3

1. Prime-time TV is the opiate of the asses.

2. Converting trash into energy may have failed, but TV producers have found a way to convert it into money.

3. The fall season has a lot in commo[n]
   Thanksgiving: It's a time when turk[...]
   to avoid getting axed.

4. You can tell TV's still in its infancy: Why
   else would viewers constantly get up to
   change the channels?

5. They call television a medium because
   nothing is ever well done, and if it is, it's
   rare.

TEMPER   *See* EMPLOYERS 2, EUROPE 2

1. People who constantly blow a fuse are usually in the dark.

2. The reason so many people fly off the
   handle is that they have a screw loose.

THE TEN COMMANDMENTS

See CLERGY, RELIGION, NYMPHOMANIACS 6

1. You know the world's in trouble when it takes 2,000 laws to enforce the Ten Commandments.

2. If the Ten Commandments were handed down today, they'd be challenged in court as discriminating against sinners.

3. The problem with many televangelists is that they follow the Ten Commandments without ever managing to catch up to them.

THANKSGIVING

See CHRISTMAS, NEW YEAR'S EVE, TELEVISION 3

1. Thanksgiving is a day when the turkey gets stuffed in the morning and the family in the afternoon.

TOUPEES

See VANITY

1. For most people, a toupee is a top secret.

TRAINS

See AUTOMOBILES, COMMUTING, TRAVEL

1. It used to be, that you had to run to catch a train. Today, if you run, you can beat it.

2. The reason trains are air conditioned is that they finally gave up trying to pry open the windows.

3. Truth is, the worst train robbery of the century is what they charge for fares.

4. Never race a train across the tracks. If you end up in a tie, you lose.

TRANSVESTITES

1. A transvestite is someone who enjoys mixed company ... alone.

2. Transvestites are mannish-depressive people who suffer from delusions of gender.

TRAVEL *See* CLOTHING 3, EUROPE 3, MOTELS 1

1. One place not to go for peace and quiet is Tibet. Everywhere you turn, it's yak, yak, yak.

2. People who take a vacation to get a tan, usually go pale when they get the bill.

3. It's one of life's contradictions that travel broadens one, but so does sitting at home on the sofa.

4. For most people, it takes two days on a cruise before they look anything like their passport photos.

5. Unfortunately, many people hate taking cruise, because it makes them cross.

6. A vacation is when a man stops doing what his boss tells him and does what his wife tells him.

7. A trip is what teaches you first-hand about the high cost of leaving.

8. A trip to the Arctic is proof positive that while many are cold, few are frozen.

9. Sightseeing is what you do till your eyes hurt. At which point some smartass tour-guide shows you a sight for sore eyes.

10. If you want to vacation cheap, just stop at a travel agency and ask where you can go. They'll gladly tell you.

11. A travel agency went out of business shortly after taking out an ad that read, "Please go away!"

TREES

See FLOWERS, BANKS 2

1. An acorn is an oak, in a nutshell.

TROUBLE

See FAILURE, LOSERS, ULCERS, THE UNITED STATES 5

1. When you're in deep water, the best thing to do is shut your mouth.

2. Life is like a shower: A wrong turn can leave you in hot water.

3. These days, the only thing guaranteed to prosper under pressure is coal.

4. If you can't be grateful for what you've received, be thankful for what you escaped.

5. It isn't the mountains that trip people up, but the molehills. / stone in your shoe

6. And it's not just the ups and downs that make life difficult, it's the jerks.

7. Most people have no trouble making ⟨ends⟩ meet: Their feet are always in their mouths.

8. Most people who moan that they don't get what they deserve should be grateful.

9. In conclusion, it's better to sleep on something before doing it, than to do it wrong and stay awake worrying.

UGLINESS   *See* BEAUTY, WALLFLOWERS

1. Ugly women who've tried to get a man to no avail should try one thing more: wearing one.

2. Ugly is when you cut off your nose and it doesn't spite your face.

3. True ugliness is when a Peeping Tom looks in your window—and reforms.

4. An ugly woman is one to whom any man who looks back looks great.

ULCERS

See YES-MEN 3

1. An ulcer is a pain in the neck that dropped ...

2. ... something you get not from what you eat but from what's eating you ...

3. ... something that comes from big money: either earning it or owing it.

THE UNITED STATES

See COMMUNISM, FREEDOM

1. The U.S. can do everything any other country can, except borrow money from the U.S.

2. In the U.S., when the budget comes out even, it's odd.

3. There's one state in which you're sure to find a welcome mat: After all, everyone knows Missouri loves company.

4. A small town is a place where the ...
   if your credit's good and your d...
   isn't.

5. In the first part of the century, the U.S.
   was a melting pot. Today, it's a pressure
   cooker.

VANITY

See EGO, PLASTIC SURGERY, TOUPEES, WOMEN 1

1. A woman who fusses in front of a mirror
   calls it "vanity." Her husband calls it
   "imagination."

2. When a woman reaches middle age, she
   gives up patting herself on the back and
   starts patting herself under the chin.

3. Self-doubt can turn a man's hair gray over-
   night, and a woman's hair any color in an
   hour.

4. A man's hair will be white as long as he
   lives. A woman's will be black as long as
   she dyes.

5. You can tell a vain man or woman: There's a mirror on the bathroom ceiling so they can admire themselves while they gargle.

6. Vain people who give up eyeglasses look better, but they don't look as well.

WALLFLOWERS *See* UGLINESS, DATING 2, 17

1. A wallflower is someone who comes home from a dance wearing the same lipstick she went with . . .

2. . . . who puts on a sweater to stay warm . . .

3. . . . whose phone doesn't even ring when she's in the bathtub . . .

4. . . . who is destined to marry a guy with a million dollars, provided she has that much.

5. A woman becomes a wallflower when she cries wolf once too often.

6. A wallflower is a woman with an infectious smile: Men see it and get ill.

7. The fact is, some wallflowers have what men would kill for: broad shoulders and a thick moustache.

8. Sadly, when a wallflower makes tea, even the kettle won't whistle.

WATCHES *See* WORK 16

1. A watchmaker is someone who doesn't charge extra for working over time.

2. Giftwise, of course, there's no present like the time.

WEALTH *See* MONEY, PHILANTHROPY, SUCCESS

1. Extravagance is a word to describe how other people spend their money.

2. The upper crust is a place where a lot of crumbs stick together.

3. The sad thing is, people born with a silver spoon in their mouth's seldom cause a stir.

4. People who spend too much time worrying about their station in life will often be told where to get off.

5. Ever notice how the toast of the town is usually the person with the most bread?

6. Status seekers are people who buy big swimming pools, then can barely keep their heads above water.

WEDDINGS
See ENGAGEMENTS, HONEYMOONS, MARRIAGE, MARRIAGE LICENSES, INFIDELITY 7

1. A wedding is a funeral where you can smell your own flowers ...

2. ... a ritual in which a woman cries during and a man afterwards ...

3. ... where a man loses complete control of himself.

4. The exercise that changes peoples' lives most is a walk down the aisle.

WIDOWS

1. A widow is someone who knows all about men, while the men who know all about her are dead.

WINE

1. It's true that wine improves with age: The older you get, the more you like it.

WOMEN

1. It's the women wearing padded bras and getting nose jobs who usually ask where all the real men have gone.

2. If you want to find out why they're called the opposite sex, just state your opinion.

3. A young woman is someone with a figure that speaks for itself. A middle-aged woman is someone with a figure that ad-libs.

4. A man talking is a monologue. A woman talking is a catalogue.

5. A man can make up his mind to stay home only if a woman hasn't made up her face to go out.

6. A tramp is a woman that men pick up, not out.

7. We men are no match for women.

8. A woman who is well reared shouldn't wear jeans.

9. Women who swear they've never been made love to have every right to swear.

10. A woman is someone whose history is often determined by her geography.

11. The secretary was anything but absent-minded when she left her clothes in the office and took the married boss to the cleaners.

12. Learning that her millionaire boss was fond of hunting, another secretary boldly approached him and announced that she was game.

13. A golddigger is someone who defies the law of gravity: She's easier to pick up than to drop.

14. She's also someone who gets her mink the same way a mink does ...

15. ... and is looking for a man to spend with the rest of her life.

16. A woman who lies about her age is like a car: The paint job may hide some wear and tear, but the lines tell the years.

17. Most women find it easy to meet men if they show themselves in the right places.

18. Of course, many women don't care for a man's company—unless he owns it.

19. It doesn't take most women long to catch a wealthy guy. Just a little wile.

20. If you don't think women are explosive, try dropping one.

21. Women are people who don't admit their age; men are people who don't act it.

22. Rule of thumb: A woman stops telling her age when it starts telling on her.

23. A woman goes from being someone a man can't get off his mind to someone he can't get off his hands.

24. To put it another way, it's better to have your hands on a woman than vice versa.

WORK *See* BUSINESS, EMPLOYERS, YES-MEN

1. Most people work for a good cause: 'cause they need the money.

2. Most employers are in the novelty business: It's a novelty when their people work.

3. The work ethic isn't what it used to be: required.

4. Today, the only real labor question you hear is, "Is it five o'clock yet?"

5. Most people enjoy having their work cut out for them ... entirely.

6. A professional rival is someone who will slap you on the back to your face, and slap you on the face behind your back.

7. And many other people are nothing more than human kites: They rise thanks to a lot of wind and some pull.

8. Actually, most people aren't afraid of hard work. They fight it year after year.

9. As a result, many workers today rust on their laurels.

I didn't rest on my laurels, I

10. Conversely, overachievers are people who walk in their sleep, so they can get their rest and their exercise at the same time.

11. Today, smart employees are those who spend December working their fingers to the bonus.

12. She's the laziest thing on earth, but her boss gave her a raise since her snoring keeps the other employees awake.

13. The second-laziest worker on earth is the one who joined as many unions as he could, to make sure he was always on strike.

14. Also pathetic is the worker who can't tell the difference between working up steam and working in a fog.

15. Ever notice how people who are waiting for something to turn up rarely start with their shirt sleeves?

16. Workers would do well to take a lesson from clocks: They pass the time by keeping their hands busy.

17. The reason most people don't recognize opportunity is that it's disguised as hard work.

THE WORLD

1. The world is something that went from being flat to round to crooked.

1. A bootlicker is someone who stoops to concur.

2. A yes-man is someone who kisses his boss on the cheeks . . .

3. . . . who always says, "Yes, sir," avoids, "No, sir," and ends up with an ul-cer . . .

4. . . . who is always letting off esteem . . .

5. . . . whose remarks are not candid, but candied . . .

6. . . . who pulls himself up by his boot-licks . . .

7. . . . who does everything the herd way . . .

8. . . . who spends more time shining up to the boss than polishing off work . . .

9. . . . who subscribes to the theory that it isn't who you know, it's who you yes . . .

10. ... who puts his best foot forward, only after making sure he won't step on the boss's toes ...

11. ... who, when he laughs at the boss's jokes, isn't after a lift but a raise.